The Visible Planets

The Visible Planets

ISBN: 978-1-7324986-7-9

Cover design by Sam Cush.

Edited by Liv Mammone and Josh Savory.

Formatted by Josh Savory.

Game Over Books
www.gameoverbooks.com

thank you to those who were with me when this project started:
joyce peseroff, kate glavin, bob sykora, emily jaegar, and august smith.

thank you to those who encouraged me throughout its development:
jill mcdonough, lloyd schwartz, zack bond, cassandra de alba, joe torra.

thank you to the folks from the salem writers group, to richard
zombeck for the copy of his father's book that contributed to many of
these poems, and to all of the people who lived these poems with me.

Table of Contents

apsides

Our Lovers

Pluto - dedicated, revering, rebuffed

Charon - much less massive than Pluto though neither would ever guess it

Jupiter - has seventy-nine known moons & herein are only the stories of three

Callisto - second only to Ganymede in Jupiter's eyes

Uranus - frozen inside

Ariel - hangs too close, recently volcanic but hiding it

Saturn - gaseous yet massive, unsure of where her surface ends & all her moons begin

Helene - fleeting, all pictures of her develop in greyscale

Io - painted face, extremely volcanic

Neptune - cobalt. genuine, but sad

Triton - permanently in retrograde, nearing a circular orbit, doomed

Eris - the first dwarf planet, throws everything into reconsideration

Dysnomia - dark, but loyal. Eris's only moon

Mars - the most relatable atmospherically, needs to be told to *grow up*

Phobos - battered, oblong, fearful, impulsive

Ceres - the largest asteroid in the belt, singular, sculpted by her own gravity

Pan - tiny, unpredictable, full of shit

Galatea - mostly rubble, waiting to be carved

Ganymede - the largest moon in the solar system, adored, darling

And though now it is hovering darkly over me
It'll look just like heaven when I get up and leave

—Waxahatchee, "Catfish"

aphelion

Description of the Hubble Space Telescope

First periscope. The best
pair of bifocals we've ever built.

Weather-eye in the astronomer's
sky. Catcher of star spills.

Cosmology teacher. School bus
with the best view in the galaxy.

The most productive scientific instrument
ever. My favorite 90s baby.

Filterer of errant space-noise. First
organism to develop sight.

Dark room orbiting Earth. Extraterrestrial
reflective chamber of light.

Comet spy. Nebula of numbers.
Slowly rotating mirror-creature.

Time determiner. Beginning definer.
Harbinger of dark matter.

Always the first to see.

My History with Stars

When I was a baby, my mom
spoon-fed me stars instead of peas.
There's a picture of me in my high chair
with light dripping in globs off my chin,
the tray a shimmering mess.

By first grade, I'd graduated from hydrogen
to chicken nuggets but now I had nebulas blooming
in my belly. I rocketed around my class room,
the shine bubbling out of my eyes.

I didn't know for a long time, but I felt them
like fingers reaching out from my body
to grip the world and wrench it towards me.
I felt the energy clamoring against the inside of my skin.

In middle school, my stars started to ricochet
from my arms to my legs, trying to become one
or forming a constellation, I don't know,
but they knocked me off balance all the time
and once, one got stuck in my heart
like an aching wad of gum.

In college, I started unconsciously wearing
a lot of red. I didn't realize that meant
I was choking until it was too late.

I was in bed for three days, sweating.
A super nova inside a body is about as outwardly
significant as one in the sky. Maybe you see it.
Maybe you were looking the wrong way.

The average person is made up
of so many black holes. The pupils,
the esophagus, the closed fist.
So what if I have one more in my gut?
I eat a little more than others,
I weigh a little more. My yawns
last longer, and I can stave off sunrise
for about six minutes.

Hubble Captures the Ghost of Cassiopeia

Here the queen is seen with her hair
piled high, frosty blue wisps pinned together,
her robes pooling on the sky-floor, swirled
around the seat of her throne. Her cheeks hold
a blush of laugher, her skin pricked with rose gold jewels.
She looks flawless underneath Polaris,
her shroud loose about her shoulders
like she hurries nowhere, dresses for no one.

We wonder where in this picture is the ghost?
Most would tell us it's the light spread of frosting,
the iridescent river nearest the edge that mimics a body.

But what if the ghost is the biggest dark spot between her pale arms?
The absent center, the hole the whole image bends around?
Or what about the disparate brightest points?
The spots that bleed the camera's pupil into exes?
Anyone who's held a death knows how infinite
it becomes, light-years of hydrogen sparks in a dark sky.

Henri Poincare's Chaos Theory

This article is telling me what planet trajectories
have in common with circadian rhythms & I'm trying
to listen to the numbers about the fractal, determined
nature of the ellipses our bodies wobble in space-time.
The same math can tell us why some people rest
fitfully while others slip under & stop breathing.
Each of us rocking ever more strange circles & how
we rotate is all here, I just need to read it.

Math can tell me exactly when & how
but the instrument of calculation: the human
brain & all of its creations are imprecise,
too rudimentary, too rounded to yield correct
answers. Instead, I can draw small ripples
around certain kinds of cancer, vibrations
of violent crashes, little rings around revolvers.
I can draw three bodies in the sand & say maybe.

The chaos theory is that our strings of numbers
will never be long enough. The answer exists,
it's reverberating in space right now, but we
will never know enough to see it still.

We could know which cell, we could know
why infection, we could know how old,
which second, we could know the first moment,
the last moment, the space of time in between.
It's just that we're not big enough calculators,
so all we see are revolving scribbles on a screen,
ghosts wobbling in the sunroom, three cars
rolling through fog, me sleeping in a chair
in the waiting room at thirteen & at twenty-four,
the film skipping, blue eyes, blue eyes, a mouth-
ful of M&Ms, a mouthful of glass.

List of Known Tidally-Locked Bodies

Mercury & the Sun, the human
pupil & things we like, Pluto & Charon,
the light square on the ceiling & my still skull,
Eris & Dysnomia, storage units & anyone
who walks by them, Uranus & Ariel, the Rockport
quarries & too many of my friends' friends' friends,
me & arachnids or the arachnid-adjacent organism,
Jupiter & Callisto, my mother & the George Washington
Bridge, Mars & Phobos, my cat & the increasingly
dull view of the front lawn, Jupiter & Ganymede,
my brother and the National Mall, the screws I lost
& the look on my mother's face as she stripped
my sister's bed for the last time, Earth & Moon,
me awake, staring & the rate of our expansion.

Cosmic Dust

All the most powerful planets have rings
I've felt inexplicably further from stardust
and I realize that this isn't how orbits work.
But there is evidence that galaxies can combine
gravitational forces to slingshot black holes
through the universe like God is vacuuming.

Calculate: three times the mass of your uncle's suicide,
and the answer is in kilometers somewhere on I-95
with your father driving, bursting comets like popcorn.

My sister doesn't live on this planet.
Black holes aren't just some cosmic curiosity.
We've all participated in them, probed the edge
of something more massive than us,
ears pressed to the dome of night, begging.
Maybe Cassiopeia can help me quit smoking.

I should probably start viewing my lover
as the 90% dark matter that he is.
I should probably start accepting myself
as the 90% dark matter that I am,
both of us unknowable to ourselves.

Pluto & Charon

Pulled out one midsummer night, Pluto drifts
to the club. The mist skirts the street in waves.
A full crowd at the Black Cat mulls & shifts,
lapping at the edges of the stage.
Charon rears his head & roars. The band blares in.
Bodies crest the human sea, tip & roll.
Every rocking skull obeys the captain
as he summons the sound that breathes them whole.

Later over gingerales, Charon confesses
that singing is like getting pitched off a cliff.
Pluto squirms but hold his eyes, suppresses
the thought *watching feels like that too*. The kiss
that flutters away: a squeal of feedback,
weightlessness, tamped down as the band packs.

Jupiter & Callisto

Callisto dons the bear-hood & looks at his ass
in the mirror. It's a self-conscious joke
he's prepared for no-one to get. They'll just
think he's cute with his tail & brown Speedo.

He worries that *Jupiter IV* is stamped
on his forehead as he steps into the slick,
velvet of the room, sees his occasional
lover encircled with women on a leather couch.

Callisto finds the gin bucket, fists half
a grapefruit & crushes it into his mouth.
After the party, a couple people still lounging
stoned in the living room, Callisto watches Jupiter

twirl on the pole, trickle to the floor & ooze up.
He cat-walks to Callisto & licks into his mouth.

Avogadro's Number

I've been taxiing too long in outdated modes
of molecular density. It's hard to make progress
with old science. The number begins in indigo,
measured, scribbled out, deemed dimensionless
as the taste of salt, the shape of our bodiless children.

Revise: my elemental addiction isn't as simple
as one gram of hydrogen. I've expanded. Ditched
puffs of smoke for dead matter, from spirit to iris,
demanded the constant apply in the physical world.

Internally, we are still debating the details.
The placement of digits, X or no X, as always.
But I know enough now to estimate my relation
to the stars, how this number revolving my brain
births clusters in dark spiraled arms.

A Diagram of an Active Galactic Nucleus

Two eyes, one inside the other,
both pupils, one black hole.

One cyan iris: the accretion disk,
storage space of rocks, furniture too strange

for the new house, toys squabbled over,
matter that won't leave you alone.

Three eyes, one perpendicular, rotated
around an axis, fresh dreams of past lovers

& old cities. Four eyes, seven rays visible
on seven wavelengths, an attempt at language.

The innermost matter, beating closest to
the darkness whirls fastest,

while outer rings try to hold the tectonic
shifting of our best kept fears.

One eye: light-years wide, 400 million
miles from Earth, finally visible in my telescope,

I imagine it sounds like a pod of whales
swimming an ellipse

nose to tail, mouth to ear,
pen to paper, ear to heart.

The Planck Constant

The subatomic integration of our genetics
expressed in joule seconds or energy multiplied
by time, the collision rate of our cells against
others that are also our cells, why my eyes
are blue, why her eyes were blue, wavelength
articulation of nervousness, predisposition
for sciatica, *angular momentum.*

If our number of heartbeats are predetermined,
they echo inside this number. It circumscribes
our particles, each ticking slowly, each with
distinct odor, a hue that leans us towards or away
from various conditions, race cars looping the track,
which will emerge first?

Subatomically, there are no freak
accidents, no sickness that doesn't add up
if you understand enough math.

Saturn & Helene

Helene's lips are cracked & flaking. She pulls
Saturn into her room at the psych ward,
jokes they stole her laxatives, a mouthful,
eyes pleading pockets for smokes, some chalk quartz.

In a field, Helene puffs a joint & lolls
in Saturn's lap, grinning. That's the day we
tell her we've never seen less of a lesbian,
and she just smiles between her friend's knees.

At dawn, Saturn lies awestruck underneath
her, world bound to the curve of ceiling fan,
the circle of Helene's arms as she sheets
off her shirt, the grey light making ghosts of her breasts.

Saturn knows there is no place safer than this:
the master bedroom of a stranger's house.

The Roche Limit

There is an invisible but finite
field surrounding a planet
in which satellites can not survive.

The gravitational force within
it bursts comets like popcorn,
scatters matter like glitter.

Beyond this line, debris floating
in the cosmos will coalesce,
indiscriminately sucked together
forming any and all objects,

but one foot to the left
moons crumble to sand, become
a rainbow of red and brown.

It is a mathematical promise
that within 2.4 times your radius is oblivion
for all who surround you.

& I'm not saying that I am any moon,
just that I've calculated
how close I can get.

Gay-Lussac's Law
(Egg in a Bottle)

I suck you into me & hold you precious, ovo
like some slick gem, a squirmy moon-particle
in my sunken snow globe. Why are you here?
Why are you tottering moist ellipses in my
bottle-brain? It is bad science to say:
tiny fire is snuffed by up-close & pimply ghost,
huge face plugging up my only glimpse of sky,
tiny bowl of ashes that is my brain, void

of cooling gases, I suck at anything face-shaped,
at anything dimpled or sickly looking
that might slide easily down my squirrelly neck
& into my gut. What my eighth grade chemistry
teacher left out, the real important science question
here, is how do you get the egg out?

Chasing Our Expansion

The most recent calculation freshly published
gets us no closer to the speed of our expansion.
I understand more about the universe through
my sister, when chemo renders her infertile.

Hubble calculated 500 kilometers per second per megaparsec,
way too fast according to recent findings, or 100 miles
an hour per million light years, or not fast enough
to catch the curly-haired, blue-eyed nieces I will never know.

The trick about this number is it can tell us how lost we are,
but not from where. Hubble's Constant defines no center
of the universe. No location of our last prick of eye contact,
or their last breath of sex, only how fast the body crumbles

away and is gone. Unchanged if you are leaping
on Pluto or plummeting past Cepheus.

Jupiter & Io

Jupiter can deadlift 405
for reps. He can't restrain his gaze from the man
in yellow, his shirt slipping glimpses as arms rise,
his shoulders fresh cut grapefruit rolling, smooth and

tart, a pool in Jupiter's mouth.
He's used to getting anything he makes
eyes at, but this has been going on for weeks.
Jupiter adjusts his Under Armor

& focuses on what he's pulling from
the floor, his brain the fizz at the top of a can
of Coke when he stands. He hopes but doesn't look.
The kid is watching his back crease between his shoulder blades.

Jupiter knows nothing about him except
his tattoos—black birds & script across his chest.

Hubble Views a Galaxy Fit to Burst

Clusters, bright birth, all
the way to the edges, clusters
tinted energetic in the constellation
of the Air Pump, host of orbiting
ancients, youth in orange bowls.

The underbelly is rose, two
scar-flesh cheeks in the midst
of uncoordinated & spasming
eyes opening, burning hot
as hyacinth, ramshackle, not
even egg-shaped, full & violent
for fifty million years of explosive
beginnings, they're blue from it.
They're punctured rubber run over,
a scatter plot saying nothing.

perihelion

Eclipse

$$t = a * i + b * s$$

A child pokes a pin
through a cardboard box, drapes
the opposite panel in white.
She is preparing.

In the days before my sister died,
she lied drugged, intubated
stuck somewhere behind watery
blue eyes. But we knew
she was there.

The doctors shined
a light into her, watched her pupils
pin. We exhaled.

The safest way to view
an eclipse is through a tiny hole.
At the right second, an image
projects and we are saved
from direct sunlight.

I was in Massachusetts again,
sleeping. My brother called, said
she was bleeding in her brain.

Overnight, which cell
let go first? At what exact moment
did the eclipse begin?

List of Likely Tidally-Locked Bodies

Neptune & Galatea, cigarette burns & our current
comforter, half-empty gallons of water & mushrooms
in my carpet, cornfields & kids on acid, Uranus & Juliet,
the song "Shooting Star" by Bad Company & the inescapable
circle of the kitchen table, dogs & smaller dogs, golf balls
& that little creek we used to catch frogs in, half-empty
handles of vodka & my hamper, Saturn & Helene,
my cat's urine & the bathroom rug, fruit cake
& gross little flies, paint chips, sharpie
markers & my everlasting self-pity,
squinting at ghost crickets under
the toilet at two a.m. & al-
cohol abuse, my cup of
dark & the sky

Neptune & Triton

It's June when Triton bursts onto the stage
of Neptune's tragedy. She's living in her
parents' crumbling basement, & he knows the words
to "Oh, Comely," can tune a guitar by ear.

Nightly, Triton exits by the sliding
glass door & treads the backyard after tucking
Neptune in, naked & nodding out.
One night he winds his red Miata to the walking

bridge in New Hope the day before the full moon.
Every spider from the woods adorned
the trusses, fat rumps like grey pearls dripping from strands
of glitter in the face of a moon with a sickle missing:

two blinks shy of tomorrow, Triton tried,
two drops out of the bucket of Neptune's eyes.

Hubble Images Milky Way's Big Sister

The picture is up close, like up her nose,
like we're still a baby in her eyes & don't know how
to frame a shot, how to back off a little.

Instead we're treated to the truth of her,
skin tone, the strands of hair that make up her head,
the crystalline wishes that stud her eyes, capillaries
that ring them, what broke in her & why.

Maybe Hubble's just examining the way she does
her eye shadow, how creamy & full of sparkles,
how tender her hand as she paints it in place,
maybe this is how Hubble wants to remember her:

this close, this age.

Eris & Dysnomia

Eris lifts her head, fumbles a Pall Mall
from the Ritz and Tums on the milk crate. Last
night's laughs, skipping firecrackers at all
the D.C. roofs, their gunshot cackles splash
inside her temples as she smokes. A smirk
twists Discord's lips. She probes around
her orbit for Dysnomia, feels her
bend over their bird cage with an apple.

How do Discord and Lawlessness unwind?
With Minor Threat's *Out of Step*, dirty chai,
and *Gone in Sixty Seconds*. Eris swipes
underneath the pillow, and a butterfly
blade skitters to the floor. She chides her wife:
We agreed. No weapons in bed, even knives.

The Stefan-Boltzmann Constant

The symbol for it is lower case sigma.
If it were uppercase it would describe the sum of everything,
but it's not. It's not quite the sum of everything,
or it's the sum of a lot of things.

$$\sigma = 2\pi\, k_B^4 \,/\, 15\, h^3 c^2 \quad \text{where:}$$

k_B is birthplace, coordinates, parenthood, element of origin,
environment or the Boltzmann constant un-meddled, energy
at the particle level

h is the Planck constant or how far in life we got
until our first major trip to the hospital. Her knee surgery
at fifteen, her body on the stretcher in the living room
at eighteen, me not yet.

ή is the reduced Planck constant: general wellness,
pallor, gastrointestinal health.

R is the universal gas constant, the firing and misfiring
of cells in the body & its ability to cannibalize.

N_A is the Avogadro constant or her draw to the city
of Boston, how she named the CITGO sign her new North Star,
and later: bandanas on her bald head under her Red Sox cap.

A(r)e is the relative atomic mass of the electron
or if our lives have meaning.

M_V is the molar mass constant or my resistance
as a younger sibling to follow the older.

R_∞ is the Rydberg constant or the number of cigarettes
I will smoke in my life time which includes while
she had cancer as well as after she died.

∝ is the fine structure constant, the value
of the affinity between me and myself. If I can hold on
or not expressed in bottles of amber.

c is the speed of light or the number of days
we will mourn.

And this finds us the radiation density of any body,
how rapidly it increases and why it can decrease,
how to determine the amount of heat a body
will give off in a life time, or why another needs
no radiation at all.

The End of a Tetrad

The faucet dripping in the night, the sun
breaching the stubborn darkness of my room,
the ocean crashing, fresh bird shit, a kid
popping from a pile of maple leaves.

The last two years held four consecutive
total lunar eclipses, brown blood moons.
Beginning a month before she died, they end
tonight. NASA calls that a tetrad.

For a while, everything was the pool
of blood in my sister's head. A crushed strawberry,
the tea bag steeping steadily, a squirt
of ketchup, a stain on someone else's shirt,
syrup expanding on a stack of pancakes,
an egg frying in a pan, the broken yolk.

Notes on the Hubble Constant

i.

no 'x' in space, no pinpoint, prick, coordinate
location, sonar, Google maps, roving hands in the dark
can't find it because it's not there

ii.

the last time you, as you, a soul attached to a body, peered
out from the inside & beheld me, the last time we connected,
pupil to pupil, & I knew for sure it was you

iii.

when she was failing, they had sex & there was a time
that was the last time. did they know it? did their hands
spasm, did they touch each others' wet faces?
could they come?

iv.

the speed at which we are leaving each other is the same
as the Hubble constant, or the same as everything else
in the universe, we just can't see it. no one can
seem to calculate it right

v.

how sickness swells in the body like maggots
squirming in a wound, which of them, bellies full,
birthed black wings and ate her whole

Mars & Phobos

It's New Year's & Mars tips a Twisted Tea
to her lips & tries not to think about
the other places Phobos would rather be.
The dude she wants had other plans worked out.

Instead, Mars is living in last week
when Phobos slid her ass slowly across
Mars's hips in the back of some kid's Jeep.
Quarter of twelve, they're alone & silent.

In school, they lie in the hallway, taking turns
staring down each other's shirts, exposing
each other's stomachs and scrawling inside jokes.
It's torture, but in the thrilling high school sense.

At midnight they sit, sipping, each pretending
separate things. At 12:03 Phobos says *fuck it* & leans in.

Ceres

Ceres insists she's asexual at best
dipped a toe in long enough to birth the Earth
& that's it. But she's been begging me for years
to write her a poem, like this is the kind of love

she yearns for. I make things in the slanted
morning light between blinds. This means
more than sitting on a curb with you outside
a dance tent the first time you tripped on acid,

more than going to Warped Tour when we're too old,
more than me hammered & stealing Hot Pockets
from your coffin freezer the night I got kicked
out of my house. We drank your father's rum

& I ate you out on the stairs of your pool
for as long as I could hold my breath.

The Rydberg Constant

can be expressed by the following equations:

$$R_\infty = \alpha^2 m_e c / 4\pi\hbar = \alpha^2 / 2\lambda_e = \alpha / 4\pi a_0$$

where R_∞ is the number of inhalations of cigarette
smoke my brain demands in my life time (λ).

m_e is the bench at the park down the street
from our house where my mother used to smoke
when her daughter & wife were fighting.

h is the Planck constant or how many head colds
and upper respiratory infections we get
in degrees of severity.

$\hbar$ is the reduced Planck constant or my current
level of forgiveness, for myself and others.

c is the speed of light in a vacuum or the average
number of cigarettes my mother and I touched, imagined,
and denied between the ages of eighteen and now.

e is the electric charge of the electron, the pull,
the chemical, the relief fizzing in my brain.

α is the fine structure constant, the strength
of the electromagnetic interaction between my throat
and the Evan Williams bottle, the amount
of time I stay drunk, continue to smoke, ignore.

λ is the wavelength of the stratospheric humming
of my sobriety, and if I can picture her death from here.

f_c is the frequency of the electron, the orbital interaction
between my frantic pace & the awareness of my actions.
I'm chain-smoking in bed, I'm dumping the ashtray
on my shirt, I'm grimy, I'm guilty & I reek.

ω_c is the angular frequency of the electron, the temperature
of my sister's infected body.

a_0 is the mean number of times my mother & I have promised
each other we will quit & meant it.

r_e is the probability of lung cancer in women who smoke.

E_n is which of us will be first.

Ludwig Boltzmann's Entropy Formula

$$S = k_B \ln W$$

Entropy is stated like a question, two
interlocking question marks, yet so certain
that we move towards it like smooth static,
the sand shaken, sifted into a flat plane when still
the current state & the eventual goal we don't know yet.
The value is S, the formula is carved
on his gravestone.

Either I already get it or I never will.

The first deciding factor is a constant
expressed in joules per Kelvin: energy
divided by temperature. Our units will always
be our potential movement divided by our internal
heat until it is bound to a unit of mass or substance,
the entropy of my cup of coffee, the grams
of my little finger, this pile of sugar.

The trickiest part here is the W, the probability,
the thermodynamic number of possibilities
for the organization of this system. We look
at his body in the ground, his tombstone.
We can only say here are the million ways
he could possibly be arranged, the S number
that describes his current state, he could be
anything. He could be anywhere. And yet
he told us how to find him.

Saturn & Pan

The first thing Saturn is told of Pan is stay
away, *bad news*, that she shakes when she doesn't drink,
& she rarely shakes, & Saturn's all *let's fucking go*.
Pan twists her baseball hat backwards & winks

a pierced eyebrow, follows Saturn, tongue first
to the rooftop, their first kiss in between black outs.
What follows is no surprise, a handle of Old Grand-dad
& a strap-on in her Jansport, selling her husband's weed

out of their basement, Pan's all legs spread & leaning,
Saturn full of afternoon vodka, in fishnets & pink
shorts, smokes a cigarette, smug. When they break
up, Pan goes wild, smashing her face into walls,

black eye, bruised ribs, walks away from
the hospital to come to Saturn's door.

The Schwarzschild Radius

My brother & I as kids, playing
Magic the Gathering on the floor of his bedroom,
that had been my bedroom,
that had been her bedroom.
I play the card of the Door to Nothingness
and the game ends abruptly.

My brother & I in Istanbul, wandering
the market. Me: marveling
at the carved ivory faces, him: searching
for what she might have bought
if she were with us.

My brother & I in Austria, eating
schnitzel with cranberry compote.
In every church he lights a candle.

There is an exact distance at which
all is lost to a black hole.
Nothing escapes, not a radio
wave, a hiccup, or the color blue
can cross that boundary.

My brother & I on the phone, he says,
You need to come back now. We'll wait for you.
He has been awake all night in the hospital
with our sister. I imagine the words, his face
when the doctor told him about the bleeding.

There were five of us in the family
we all knew what we were approaching.
we got close, orbited, turned away.

We let him spend the night inside of it alone.

Energy Conversions

erg, joule, foot-pound,
calorie, horsepower-hour,
kilowatt-hour, energy of fission
of one atom

energy equivalent of one ton
of TNT, hydrogen fusion,
energy equivalent of one gram
of matter.

ton of coal, cord of red oak,
one hundred gallons of fuel oil,
twenty thousand cubic feet
of natural gas.

United States energy consumption
(projected 1970-2000),
Earth's daily receipt of solar
energy, Earth's total heat content,
one D-cell flashlight battery

apsides

The Soft Capture Mechanism

On the fifth & final service mission to Hubble,
the astronauts replaced all of the eighteen-year-old
batteries, installed a new spectrograph, a third massive
camera, the most advanced the telescope had ever met.
They polished it up real nice, dusted its ears off, brushed
its teeth, combed the meteor-matter out of its hair,
& wrapped it all up in a fresh thermal blanket.

Who knows how long it could keep on shuttering
away up there, clicking off rounds of pictures of bygone
stars, twirling its gyroscopes underneath the moon?

When they left, Hubble saw in ultraviolet
for the first time, that frantic singing above the spectrum
of visible light, impossible for us, but Hubble
reads it loud and clear, hears the human advancement
in its tone, this new tenor of space-ray, an uncharted
landscape murmuring in the distance. Hubble barely notices
they've gone, it's so thrilled with its bells & whistles,
it goes through each of them, listening with
this one & peering out with that one. It shrugs its
shoulders around trying to reach something bolted
to its back, but it can't quite. What use could it be
if it's not between Hubble & the heavens?
This strange metal ring doesn't seem
good for anything.

Eclipsing Binaries

By observing how two stars orbit each other
we can know the point that binds them.
From light years away, we can look at their union
and say this, this is what makes them partners.

Never mind that we can't know their names,
or the language in which they say, *I love you.*
We can feel the way their light shifts and dodges
as they dance, see their alternating rhythm as they
wash dishes, get dogs, fix the fence in the front yard.
We can't tell their faces apart at this distance,
yet we know beyond a doubt which will die first.

We know their collected mass, the length of their arms,
the moment their first child is stillborn, the brightness
of their mourning, and the time at which it will end:
swollen, red, cold, and bigger than both of them.

Uranus & Ariel

Years later at a diner by the navy base,
Ariel is stoned and picking at her fraying jeans.
She orders two eggs scrambled like always.
Uranus has dyed her hair jet black and seems

like crumbling clay. She limps & has a cane.
She eats creamed chipped beef, her voice a whisper.
She was bone-sick, bed-bound, her mother proclaimed
kidnapped. She took a taxi to the E.R.

and took a taxi home. What good are you,
Ariel? She's the first girl you shaved your
pussy for. You're not sixteen and kissing
in the dark room of your high school anymore.

She's now divorced & stitched together inside.
You couldn't protect her. You didn't even try.

Science Has Some Shitty Answers for My Questions

Geologically, the moon is dead.

I guess I've never really expected
the moon to be alive, but it still comes
as a shock to hear it's dead.

This sucks. The moon's dead but
I can still fucking see her, hung in the sky.
I used to think she smiled at me sometimes,
but now it looks like this haunted grin.
I used to paint my face & take to the fields
every twenty-eight days but now what?
I can honor her ghost every month?

I'd rather someone just pull the cord
& shut her out than all of us
stand here, mouths open, watching
her serene body float through a still pool.

No Scientist Has Ever Suggested That Dark Matter Is the Universe Digesting Itself

but the planets know that somewhere
closer to the edge there is an open mouth
drooling stardust in phosphorescent dollops
from gravitationally detectable teeth.

What if we all understood
our rotation: a carnival ride on roller skates
whirling down an unknowable drain.

Carl Sagan said *we are*
a way for the cosmos to know itself.

*

The scientist triangulating the weight
of a system of stars
has extra.

My sister at twenty-three gulps
radio-active solution
has extra.

*

I've seen bodies revert to hydrogen
marched away slowly over years
as if by galactic ants hanging
a constellation of loss.

I've surrendered as a part of the organ.
Everything rends itself inside
a bulging stomach of stars.

Hubble's Letter to the James Webb

At first, be a blunder.
Be a disappointment, fool
them. Make them think you
no different than a space rock
filled with diamonds. Make them puzzle
over you, give them the gift of problem
solving. Let them generate the feat of
human engineering that fixes you.

Then, tell them what they want to hear
in all its wispy, pinprick detail. Let them
be amazed, marvel at the least you can do.
If they ask for the beginning, tell them
it's possible, but they'll have to conjure it,
sit at your feet & pray long enough in the right
numerical combinations. Make them sweat and then
drop the cloak of darkness from the universe's shoulders.

Reveal to them their secrets: that everyone
has children, even if we don't know them, that
everyone orbits, that shadows lurk under ice,
that stars mock the shape of each of our faces,
that even emptiness has a name and pulls us.

When you are more than they have ever dreamt,
keep clicking. Show them you are just getting started.
It will be like magic for them, better than God explaining.
You can show them millions of years of proof of ghosts,
you can display almost impenetrable depths and what crawls
there. You can whisper to them their only great hope:
that they might not be alone, that one morning they will
wake up to an image of a hand waving *hello*.

Neptune & Galatea

On the walk to the party Galatea jokes
that the only ocean she has eyes for will
be hers tonight and cites that time they almost
kissed: the bathroom, some house by the Bookmill.

The group arrives at a loft spilling people,
a pile of PBRs that missed the can.
By ten thirty, she learns that Neptune wields
a blue dildo, that the name "Earth-Shaker" isn't

about horses. As Tea's pulling up her pants,
Neptune picks up a Polaroid says *Can I?*
In the picture, she's topless, looking away.
She's sober now—a statue come alive.

Neptune watched her on her first shaky day
while she twisted sea beasts out of clay.

Planck's Constant (revisited)

$$E = h \, f$$

the quantum of action, the translator, the quotient we filter
our vernacular through, preceding every sentence, every plea

we're locked in space with it, I think I have my own & you
have yours, but physics says they're all the same, my arc-second

the number between the twitch of our blinking, our inhalation
of movement, the *minimal increment of energy*, the witching

instant of my fickle favors, the *electrical charge of an oscillator
in a cavity*, the ticking & unsure warbling tapping in my cavern

this is the one—the constant that exists to transpose the frequency
of our swaying into the amount of hope we cycle with

some might look & say it all depends on wavelength, speed
of light, but I will tell you in my science the determining

factor is the frequency of us returning, the touch
of your cheek to mine, my cheek to yours

Description of the Hubble Space Telescope (cont.)

Imaging an unreddened star
in order to achieve ratio, exposure,
assuming low-background conditions.

The visual is strongly affected by the sky.

Near the center, assume clear quartz,
spectroscopy, signal-to-pixel, multiple
values corresponding respectively.

If in range, entries transfer in faint

points, little sky, significant losses.
Three are exposed simultaneously,
arranged in an "L" shape, covering a field.

Is the dispersion first? Order

slits the prism. All modes can be operated
by replacing a clear aperture, low-resolution
spectra, various locations in the linear ramp.

Jupiter & Ganymede

Jupiter downplays the extent of his
gang ties as long as he can. The first time
he's shirtless near Ganymede, his chest tattoos
ring the room like the presence of his skin,

the inkling of touch, an internal flood.
Sometimes they fight, shove each other, smoke-hole,
grapple & tackle each other, no blood,
Jupiter's eyes all moon-shark & crescent roll.

The guns appear, stolen cars, & nights of black
splatter on his shoes when he finally shows,
hours late, Ganymede with tears choked back
as Jupiter lists the steps to dispose

of a body. He hangs grinning from Ganymede's
skylight, taunting, then flops onto his sheets.

Ludwig Boltzmann's Entropy Formula (revisited)

I intended to organize my life, but I spent
the morning studying thermodynamics instead.
Turns out, I had no chance anyway. Because what is life
if not a series of spontaneous processes
continually increasing the entropy
of our macro-state?

Even if our macro-state is both of us
in the house, our micro-state on any given
minute could be:
    you on the toilet, me eating oatmeal
    you making pesto, me reading Hopkins
    you hanging plastic on the windows, me
    shivering and drinking tea, us both: on
    the couch, me: trailing a foot across the floor
as each of these becomes more probable, which
they all are equally probable, our entropy increases.

I don't think they mean spontaneous as in
the thing that clicks in my brain that makes me
walk out of the house at two in the morning &
tell you to go fuck yourself, which is just as
spontaneous as the light that thrums in my brain
stem when I rub the hairs on the back of your head,
but thermodynamics insists that both of these
increase our entropy
which is honestly pretty comforting.

The Drake Equation

$$N = R * f_p * N_p * f_e * f_l * f_i * f_c * L$$

My boyfriend and I go out for tacos
to celebrate our first full revolution
around the sun together.

It is a big deal for both of us loners.
We've been leading silent civilizations
inside our bodies for years
not used to contact, starting
to doubt.

On the back of a napkin, I write him
the Drake Equation, explain:

R is all the newborn, wailing stars
having their first blazing burps
expressed as a ratio in solar masses per year

f_p stands for the fraction of stars
pirouetting hands out, palms
full of planets

N_p is the average number of planets
per star

f_e slashes the number again by
the planets that develop life, I wink
at my boyfriend to convey the beginning
of the guesstimates

f_i divides these meager lives
by those we consider intelligent

f_c provides the final axe, the fraction
of these civilizations that produce technology

finally! as if we are not yet improbable
enough, the last multiplier L, the lifetime
of a civilization in years

because two intelligent civilizations
capable of communication
is a waste if one burns out
just as the other invents the radio.

Jupiter and Three Moons

February: the snow starts and doesn't stop.
People older than me say my sister will
speak to me if I listen hard enough.

A picture of Jupiter and three moons appears.
I consider her: pale planet rubbed red and raw,
contemplating suicide every morning.

Europa, the ice queen, the smallest, on the edge,
has recently quit smoking and twirls in a fury.

The volcanic sister, Io, floating far above,
luminescent yellow, without a shadow.

We can see her only in our mother's face.

Callisto, the brown bear, the brother,
big enough to hold us all or so we think.

The song I'm listening to gets louder:
I hope my sister grows up and thinks

that the world is beautiful.
There are many moons not in this photograph.
My brother and sister could have been anyone

but they weren't. Someone took this picture,
and someone wrote this song, and Jupiter looks like
my mother and eventually it has to stop snowing.

The Third EGRET Catalogue

Me studying science goes like this: Ooh.
What a cool name. I wonder what it is.
Step one: Ask NASA. NASA says,

*The Third EGRET Catalogue consists of 271 sources: 5 pulsars, 1 solar
flare, 66 high-confidence blazar identifications, 27 possible blazar
identifications, 1 likely radio galaxy, 1 normal galaxy, & 170 unidentified
sources.*

Which means nothing to me.
So I try again, dive back in, what is it actually?
When I find what I'm looking for, it is always
a hundred pages of letters & numbers, tables
from which I understand exactly nothing.
But I marvel at them. Shake my googly eyes around
in their plastic moons at them, try to suck them in
through the alphabet filter on the front of my face.

3EG J0824-4610, 126.17, -46.18, +/- 0.07
features 68, 142, GRO J0823-46 Vela SNR

I back track. Click *Overview*. Dig my way
out of the bowels of the NASA website
for a breath of non-numerical air.

When I'm ready, click the revised table
for some more recent data. NASA says,

*The revised EGRET Catalogue details 188 sources, 14 confused, the
authors do not confirm most of the 3EG sources associated with the Gould
Belt & new error circles overlap previous ones except in Sgr A*, certain
radio galaxies, and several micro-quasars. The authors cross-correlated
the source positions with a large number of radio pulsars, wind nebulae,
supernova remnants, OB associations, blazars, and flat radio sources.*

I understand: Table of gamma ray sources.
I click: *Browse This Table*, find *Object Name*
& type in my current favorite pulsar. Here
are the coordinates for the thing in the sky
I want to listen to: [11 04 27.31, +38 12 31.8]
Click *Optical Image*. Click *X-ray Image*.
In fuzzy blue, red eyes squinting out of dense black,
a pinpoint, one blaze of dark energy filed under
Images centered on requested position.

I can see it.
On April 19th, flux
as defined by 10^8 photons/cm²/s
was 14.1. On April 24th was 19.4,
was 13.2,
was 16.8,
was 10.7,
error margin 1.8, is radiant,
error margin 3.3, is radiant,
error margin 2.4, is radiant,
and I see it, and its pulses, and its blazes
and its quantifiable highest electromagnetic frequency waves
and I'm in Massachusetts and I'm in flux
and my coordinates are [42.529, -70.9] and my red shift is ~.031,
and my error margin is 15.9, viewing period p56,
alternate name, declination, find
me, find me,
find me.

Parallax

The word means *alteration* in Greek like
dress seams, or close one eye & then the other.
The closer the flame is to your face, the more
it jumps in your vision. Which means that numbers plus
this trick of the eye can tell us the distance to stars
based on our orbit of the sun.

Imagine, you are a space beast slowly blinking,
one blue eye: the Earth's furthest point of orbit
to the right, close it, now open the other terrestrial eye
at the furthest point of orbit to the left.

Two images blaze in your telescopic mind.
Sketch a triangle on the blacktop of cosmos,
trace those two star images and your sight lines
to the position of your geo-eyes. Lastly,
draw a line from your sun through the apex
of that triangle, the location of your star.

What else can you find? If we can measure
the distance of illuminated gas from the location
of our bodies, why can't we find our dead?
Why can't we find the nights that taunt us, images
more vivid than stars? Can't we find the angle
between us and our grief? So we could finally say here,
here is where I need to stamp my foot, pitch the rock,
aim the punch, point the cross-hairs so that
this mass will be scattered into darkness.

Glossary of abbreviations and symbols used in astronomy and astrophysics

Å   Angstrom unit, 10^{-10} m

∝   right ascension, fine structure constant

AU   astronomical unit (distance), $1.495\ 979$ x 10^{11} m

b, B, β latitude (in various spherical coordinate systems)

c   speed of light, $2.997\ 924\ 58$ x 10^8 m/s

Δ   distance from Earth

δ   declination

ε   obliquity of ecliptic

e eccentricity

e   base of natural logarithm, $2.718\ 2818$; charge of electron

ET   Ephemeris time

f frequency, Earth flattening

G   Newtonian constant of gravitation

GMT   Greenwich mean time

h, t   hour angle

h   Planck's constant

H_0 Hubble constant (present day value)

J   joule, SI unit of energy (replacing the erg)

J_2 Earth's dynamical form factor

k Gaussian gravitational constant, Boltzmann constant, curvature index

kpc   kiloparsec, 10^3 pc

L luminosity, usually given in solar units

$L\odot$ solar absolute luminosity

ly light year, 9.46 x 10^{12} km

LSR   local standard of rest

λ   wavelength

M mean anomaly

M⊙   solar mass

Mpc   megaparsec, 10^6 pc

ω   angular distance of pericenter (perihelion)

Ω_0 density parameter of the present-day Universe

pc   parsec, 3.0857 x 10^{13} km

π, p parallax (arc-second)

q	perihelion distance (in parabolic and hyperbolic orbits)
R	Rydberg constant
R_0	refraction constant, radius of curvature of the Universe
p, s	angular separation (of binary stars)
P_c	present-day critical density of the Universe
σ	Stefan-Boltzmann constant
T	time of perihelion passage
T_{eff}	stellar effective temperature
t	time (sometimes also hour angle)
TAI	International Atomic Time
TCG	Geocentric Coordinate Time
TDT	Terrestrial Dynamical Time
v	true anomaly
X,Y,Z	rectangular solar coordinates in equatorial coordinate system
x, y, z	heliocentric rectangular coordinates, galactic rectangular coordinates
z	zenith distance, redshift parameter

Acknowledgements

The title *The Visible Planets* refers to the section in *The Old Farmer's Almanac* that tells us where and when to look for the planets in the night sky in the coming year.

"Description of the Hubble Space Telescope (cont.)," "Energy Conversions," and "Glossary of abbreviations and symbols used in astronomy and astrophysics" all contain found text from *The Handbook of Space Astronomy and Astrophysics* by Martin V. Zombeck.

"Hubble Captures the Ghost of Cassiopeia," "Hubble Views a Galaxy Fit to Burst," "Hubble Images Milky Way's Big Sister," and "Jupiter and Three Moons" are all titles of articles accompanying pictures published to NASA.gov.

"List of Known Tidally-Locked Bodies" draws its name from the Wikipedia article about tidal locking.

"The Third EGRET Catalogue" draws its title and numerical information from a catalogue of gamma ray sources published by The Astrophysical Journal Supplement Series, Volume 123, Issue 1, pp. 79-202.

"Hubble's Letter to the James Webb" appears on the NASA website under the public submissions for the JWST-ART project.

"List of Known Tidally-Locked Bodies" was first published in the *Oyez Review*, volume 45, Spring 2018.

"Planck's Constant (revisited)" uses language from the Wikipedia article on the Plank Constant and was first published in *Hollow 6*, by Brokentooth Press in 2019.

"Eclipse," "Cosmic Dust," "No Scientist Has Ever Suggested that Dark Matter is the Universe Digesting Itself," "The Drake Equation," and "Science Has Some Shitty Answers for My Questions" were first published in *Wyvern Lit*, Issue Five, Spring 2015.

In "Jupiter and Three Moons," the italicized lines are lyrics from the Told Slant song "In San Francisco."

Aly Pierce lives in Beverly, MA. She works at Deathwish Inc. making sure you stay in the latest vinyl and also teaches. Originally from Doylestown, Pennsylvania, she attended Hampshire College for writing, and then later UMASS Boston where she received her MFA in Poetry. She is the daughter of two lesbians and two golfers, the granddaughter of an undertaker's daughter, an astronomy teacher, a Philadelphia fireman, and the greenest thumb in the world.

You can find her on Twitter and Instagram as @instantweekend.